tage 1

Vordless Stories B

iz Miles

uided Reading Notes

The Swing Ball

The Street Fair

The Big Box

Fetch!

The Hedgehog

The Apple

Introduction

Oxford Reading Tree stories at Stages 1–4 feature settings and situations most children will find familiar. The stories reflect the experiences of most 4–6-year-olds: having a bath, going to a party, having new shoes, getting into trouble. Children of this age will readily identify with the characters and situations. This also helps build comprehension.

The wordless books at Stage 1 allow children to learn how stories work, including the order and direction in which they are read and how stories are structured, with a beginning, middle and end. Each book tells a complete story through funny and engaging pictures. All this helps to develop children's comprehension skills and also builds their confidence in their ability to read. When used alongside your systematic phonic teaching they will help children put all their reading skills into practice in a highly motivating way.

Using the books

This booklet provides suggestions for using the books for guided, group and independent activities. The reading activities include ideas for developing children's *word recognition* W and *language comprehension* C skills. Within word recognition, there are ideas for helping children practise their phonic skills and knowledge, as well as helping them to tackle words that are not easy to decode phonically. The language comprehension ideas include suggestions for teaching the skills of prediction, questioning, clarifying, summarising and imagining in order to help children understand the text and the whole stories. Suggestions are also provided for speaking, listening, drama and writing activities.

Reading fluency

To support children in developing fluency in their reading and give them plenty of opportunities to revisit the stories. This includes:

- rereading independently
- rereading with a partner
- rereading at home
- listening to audio versions of the story (e.g. Talking Stories)
- hearing the story read to them by others as they follow the printed text.

Rereading and rehearing helps children develop automatic word recognition and gives them models of fluent, expressive reading.

Comprehension strategies

Story	Comprehension strategy taught through these Teaching Notes				
	Prediction	Questioning	Clarifying	Summarising	Imagining
The Swing Ball	✓	✓	✓	✓	
The Street Fair	✓	✓	✓		✓
The Big Box	✓	✓	✓	✓	
Fetch!	✓	✓		✓	✓
The Hedgehog		✓	✓	✓	✓
The Apple	✓	✓	✓	✓	✓

Vocabulary and phonic opportunities

The chart shows the main words used in each book. The decodable words listed should be decodable for most children at this Stage. The tricky words are common but do not conform to the phonic rules taught up to this point – children will need support to learn and recognise them. If children struggle with one of these words you can model how to read it.

The Swing Ball	Decodable words	
	Tricky words	ball, swing, the
The Street Fair	Decodable words	
	Tricky words	fair, street, the
The Big Box	Decodable words	big, box
	Tricky words	the
Fetch!	Decodable words	
	Tricky words	fetch
The Hedgehog	Decodable words	
	Tricky words	hedgehog, the
The Apple	Decodable words	
	Tricky words	apple, the

Curriculum coverage chart

	Speaking, listening, drama	Reading	Writing
The Swing Ball			
PNS Literacy Framework (YF)	1.3, 1.4	W 5.1, 5.3 C 7.1, 7.3	11, 12
National Curriculum	Working towards Level 1		
Scotland (5–14) (P1)	Level A	Level A	Level A
N. Ireland (P1/Y1)	Social use of language 6 Language and thinking 1, 4, 5, 11	1, 3, 5, 6	3
Wales (Key Stage 1)	Range 1, 3 Skills 1, 3	Range 1, 4, 5, 6 Skills 1, 2	Range 2, 3, 4 Skills 2, 3, 5
The Street Fair			
PNS Literacy Framework (YF)	2.2	W 5.1, 5.2, 5.5, 5.9 C 7.1	11
National Curriculum	Working towards Level 1		
Scotland (5–14) (P1)	Level A	Level A	Level A
N. Ireland (P1/Y1)	Language and thinking 8, 10, 11	1, 3, 5, 6	3
Wales (Key Stage 1)	Range 1, 3, 5 Skills 1, 2	Range 1, 4, 5, 6 Skills 1, 2	Range 2, 3 Skills 2, 3

Key

C = Language comprehension Y = Year

W = Word recognition F = Foundation/reception

In the designations such as 5.2, the first number represents the strand and the second number the bullet point

Curriculum coverage chart

	Speaking, listening, drama	Reading	Writing
The Big Box			
PNS Literacy Framework (YF)	1.2, 2.3	W 5.1, 5.2, 5.3, 5.9 C 7.4	11, 12
National Curriculum	Working towards Level 1		
Scotland (5–14) (P1)	Level A	Level A	Level A
N. Ireland (P1/Y1)	Language and thinking 9, 11	1, 3, 5, 6	3
Wales (Key Stage 1)	Range 1, 2, 3 Skills 1, 2, 3, 4	Range 1, 4, 5, 6 Skills 1, 2	Range 2, 3, 4 Skills 2, 3, 6
Fetch!			
PNS Literacy Framework (YF)	1.1, 4.1	W 5.3, 5.8, 5.9 C 7.3, 8.2, 8.3	9.1, 12
National Curriculum	Working towards Level 1		
Scotland (5–14) (P1)	Level A	Level A	Level A
N. Ireland (P1/Y1)	Social use of language 6 Language and thinking: 3, 11	1, 3, 5, 6	3
Wales (Key Stage 1)	Range 1, 3 Skills 1, 3	Range 1, 4, 5, 6 Skills 1, 2	Range 2, 3 Skills 2, 3

Curriculum coverage chart

	Speaking, listening, drama	Reading	Writing
The Hedgehog			
PNS Literacy Framework (YF)	1.2, 1.5	W 5.1, 5.10, 5.12 C 7.1, 7.3	11.1, 12.1
National Curriculum	Working towards Level 1		
Scotland (5–14) (P1)	Level A	Level A	Level A
N. Ireland (P1/Y1)	Language and thinking 1, 8, 9, 10, 11	1, 3, 5, 6	3
Wales (Key Stage 1)	Range 1, 2, 3 Skills 2, 3, 4	Range 1, 4, 5, 6 Skills 1, 2	Range 1, 2, 3 Skills 2, 3, 5
The Apple			
PNS Literacy Framework (YF)	1.2, 3.1	W 5.2, 5.10 C 7.3, 7.4, 8.3	10.1, 11
National Curriculum	Working towards Level 1		
Scotland (5–14) (P1)	Level A	Level A	Level A
N. Ireland (P1/Y1)	Language and thinking 1, 10, 11	1, 3, 5, 6	3
Wales (Key Stage 1)	Range 1, 2, 3 Skills 2, 3	Range 1, 4, 5, 6 Skills 1, 2	Range 2, 3, 4 Skills 2, 3, 5

The Swing Ball

C = Language comprehension	*R, AF* = QCA reading assessment focus
W = Word recognition	*W, AF* = QCA writing assessment focus

Group or guided reading

Introducing the book

- C *(Questioning)* Read the title to the children. Look at the cover picture. Ask them: *Who are the children in the picture? What are they doing?*
- C *(Clarifying)* Look through the rest of the book and identify all the ball games they are playing. Ask: *What happens to the ball each time?*
- C *(Prediction)* Look at page 8. Ask: *Why do you think a swing ball is a good idea?*
- Encourage the children to talk about their own experiences of ball games and if they ever lose the ball.

Strategy check

Do the children look carefully at the illustrations and notice details?

Independent reading

- W Start with the cover again. Ask the children to point to the words as they read the title with you.
- C *(Clarifying)* Ask the children to look through the book and tell the story in their own words. Encourage them to use 'Oh no!' when the ball flies away.
- C *(Clarifying)* On page 8, ask: *Why is Dad smiling?*

Assessment Check that children:

- *(R, AF3)* are aware of the story structure, e.g. actions/reaction, consequence, and the way that the story was built up and concluded
- *(R, AF4)* open the book and 'read' it from left to right.

Returning to the text

C *(Summarising)* Ask the children to retell the story in their own words, without referring to the pictures.

W Remind the children of the title and ask them to point to each word as you read it. Ask the children to look through the book to find some of the same words in a picture (page 6).

Group and independent reading activities

Objective Show an understanding of the elements of stories, such as main character, sequence of events, and openings (7.3).

C *(Questioning, Clarifying)* Ask the children the following questions:

Can you show me the page where Biff is playing cricket?
Where does the ball go? What do you think will happen next?
How do you think the neighbour feels?
How does Dad feel?
How do Biff and Chip feel?

Assessment *(R, AF2)* Do the children scan the picture for clues to the answers to these questions?

Objective Explore and experiment with sounds, words and texts (5.1). Know that print carries meaning and, in English, is read from left to right (7.1).

You will need word cards of the words in the title: The, Swing, Ball.

C *(Questioning)* Jumble the words up and ask the children to put them in the correct sequence, explaining that the words don't make sense if they read 'Ball Swing The' or 'Ball The Swing'.

- Ask what they think of 'Swing The Ball'. Say: *It makes sense, but is it the title?*

Assessment *(R, AF1)* Do the children realise that there are three separate words in the title?

Objective Recognise letter shapes and say a sound for each (5.3).

W Write the words 'The Swing Ball' on the board.

- Ask the children to think of other types of balls and write them as a list on the board.
- Ask the children to say each word as you write them.
- Point to words randomly and ask the children to sound out the first letter of each word.

Assessment *(R, AF1)* Do the children recognise letter shapes?

Speaking, listening and drama activities

Objective Use language to imagine and recreate roles and experiences (1.3). Speak clearly and audibly with confidence and control and show awareness of the listener (1.4).

You will need a ball.

- Sit in a circle with the children and pass the ball to a child. Ask the child whether he/she has ever experienced playing with a ball and losing it. Ask: *What happened?* Encourage the child to speak loudly so that everyone can hear what they say.
- The child then passes the ball to another child who recalls any similar experience.
- Continue around the group.

Writing activities

Objective Write their own names and other things such as labels and captions (11). Use a pencil and hold it effectively to form recognisable letters, most of which are correctly formed (12).

You will need paper and a variety of pencils, crayons and coloured pencils.

- Ask the children to make a book cover about a different game Biff and Chip could play.
- Ask them to look again at the list of ball games on the board, then copy one down as the title of their book. They can write their own name as the author and then draw a picture of Biff and Chip playing the game.
- Tell the children that they can look at the cover of *The Swing Ball* to remind them how it should look.

Assessment *(W, AF8)* Are the children able to write their own names legibly and spell the words correctly?

The Street Fair

C = Language comprehension	*R, AF* = QCA reading assessment focus
W = Word recognition	*W, AF* = QCA writing assessment focus

Group or guided reading

Introducing the book

W Read the title to the children. Ask them to point to and sound out the letters at the beginning of 'street'. Read the word with the children, blending the letters.

C *(Questioning)* Talk about the picture on the cover. Ask the children: *Have you ever been to a street fair? What sorts of things happen at them? Who is going to the street fair in this story?*

C *(Clarifying)* Look through the book and identify the different activities at the street fair.

C *(Prediction)* Look at pages 6 and 7. Ask: *What do you think Dad, Chip and Biff did at the street fair? How do you know that Mum, Kipper and Floppy are surprised?*

C *(Questioning)* Look at page 8. Ask: *Who else gets his face painted?*

Strategy check

Check that the children recognise and name the characters.

Independent reading

- Ask the children to look through the book and tell the story in their own words.

C *(Imagining)* Ask them what they think Dad, Chip and Biff say on pages 6 and 7. Ask: *What do you think Mum and Kipper say?*

C *(Clarifying)* Talk about words that express surprise.

C *(Clarifying)* On page 8, ask the children to describe some of the features painted on the characters' faces. Ask: *What is Floppy wearing? Why isn't his face painted?*

Assessment Check that children:

- *(R, AF2)* notice enough information in the pictures to tell and understand the story
- *(R, AF3)* recount the story, with the main points in sequence.

Returning to the text

W On page 1, ask the children to sound out any of the letters they recognise. Point to the word 'dip' and help them to read it out by sounding out the letters in order, then blending them.

W On page 2, point to the word 'Fun' and encourage the children to sound out and blend the letter sounds.

Group and independent reading activities

Objective Hear and say sounds in words in the order in which they occur (5.5). Read some high frequency words (5.9).

You will need the sentences below written on the board:

Chip was a tiger.

Biff was a clown.

C *(Imagining)* Ask the children what they would like their faces painted as and add their names and characters to the list.

W Ask the children to say the words with you as you write them on the board, sounding and blending the phonemes.

Assessment *(R, AF1)* Are the children able to read the high frequency words quickly? *(R, AF4)* Do they understand that each sentence ends with a full stop?

Objective Explore and experiment with sounds and words (5.1). Link sounds to letters (5.2).

W Ask the children what sound a tiger makes ('Grrr'). Ask them: *What is the first sound in 'Grrr'?* Then write it on the board.

- Do the same thing for other animal noises, e.g. 'Sssss' for snake, 'Meow' for cat.

Assessment *(R, AF1)* Are the children able to associate each sound with its letter?

Objective Know that print carries meaning and, in English, is read from left to right and top to bottom (7.1).

C *(Clarifying, Imagining)* Ask the children to imagine that the school is holding a fair. Ask: *What sort of signs or posters would you need? What would they say?*

C *(Clarifying)* Turn to pages 4 and 5 and ask the children: *Can you show me the writing on this page? Can you show me the drawing? How many signs and posters can you find in the story?*

W Ask the children to look through the book and find the words 'Street Fair' written in two different ways.

Assessment *(R, AF3)* Are the children able to locate the writing automatically?

Speaking, listening and drama activities

Objective Sustain attentive listening, responding to what they have heard (2.2).

- Ask the children to describe how they would like their faces to be painted.
- Then ask one child to say three things to describe the face painting, but without saying what or who they are.
- Ask the other children in the group to guess what the face painting is. You may have to model this to the whole class first so that they understand what has to be done.

Writing activities

Objective Write their own names and other things such as labels and captions (11).

You will need a variety of drawing material: paper, crayons, or coloured pencils.

- Ask the children to draw a picture of themselves with their face painted.
- Ask them to write underneath the picture 'I am a…'

Assessment *(W, AF2)* Do they start their sentences with a capital letter and end with a full stop?

(W, AF8) Do they use correct spelling?

The Big Box

C = Language comprehension — *R, AF* = QCA reading assessment focus
W = Word recognition — *W, AF* = QCA writing assessment focus

Group or guided reading

Introducing the book

- Read the title and ask the children: *When would you say this?* Explain the exclamation mark and ask the children to read the title dramatically.
- C *(Prediction)* Read the title and look at the picture on the cover. Ask the children: *What do you think is in the big box?*
- Talk about different types of packaging. Ask the children: *Can you think of any things that come in cardboard boxes? What comes in plastic bags?*

Strategy check

Check the children notice the words in the pictures.

Independent reading

- C *(Clarifying)* Look at the first page of the story. Ask the children: *What was in the big box?*
- C *(Questioning)* On pages 6–7, ask: *Why is the playhouse falling down?*
- C *(Questioning)* On page 8, ask: *Do you think this is a better playhouse?*
- C *(Summarising)* Ask the children to look through the book again and tell the story in their own words.

Assessment Check that children:

- *(R, AF2)* notice enough information in the pictures to tell and understand the story
- *(R, AF3)* understand why the boxes collapsed.

Returning to the text

W On page 3, ask: *Can you read the words on the box?* Ask the children to sound out and blend the words in 'up'. Ask them to point to the words as you read, 'This way up'.

W On page 4, say: *Point to the words in the picture.* Encourage them to sound out and blend the letters in the word 'Floppy'. Help them to read the words 'our house'.

C *(Clarifying)* Ask children to describe what is happening on page 8. Ask: *What is Dad doing? What is Mum holding?*

Group and independent reading activities

Objective Show an understanding of the elements of stories, such as main character, sequence of events (7.3). Retell narratives in the correct sequence (7.4).

C *(Questioning)* Start by asking the children: *What happened at the beginning of the story? What happened in the middle? What happened at the end?*

- Ask the children to show you the page where the rain started. Ask: *How do you know that it is raining on this page?*
- Ask: *What happens on the next page? What happens at the end?*

Assessment *(R, AF1)* Are the children able to retell the story, putting the events into the correct sequence?

Objective Recognise letter shapes and say a sound for each (5.3). Read some high frequency words (5.9).

W Draw a big box on the board. Write the label 'This way up'. Ask children to sound out the letters they know. Add the label 'Fragile'. Talk about the meaning of the words 'fragile' and 'this way up'.

- Ask the children what other labels there could be on a big box and write them on the board, e.g. 'Open here', 'Open with care'. Ask the children to sound out and blend the letters in 'open' with you.

Assessment *(R, AF1)* Do the children quickly recognise and read the word 'up'?

Objective Explore and experiment with sounds, words and texts (5.1). Link sounds to letters (5.2).

(W) Ask the children to look at the title of the story. Ask them what sound 'big' and 'box' begin with, and what letter makes this sound. Explain that this is an example of alliteration.

- Ask the children to think up other titles which use alliteration, e.g. 'The Mighty Mouse', 'The Funny Frog', 'The Dirty Dog'.
- Can the children identify the initial sounds and letters easily? Do they understand what alliteration is and can they suggest alliterative titles?

Assessment *(R, AF1)* Do the children hear the repeated sounds and link them with the correct letters?

Speaking, listening and drama activities

Objective Extend their vocabulary, exploring the meanings and sounds of new words (1.5, 2.3).

- Ask one child to explain to the others in the group how to make a playhouse out of a big box.
- Write 'The Big Box' on the board and ask the children to think up a funny sentence using words beginning with 'b', e.g. 'The big box bounced on the boy and gave him a bump'.
- Take the word 'big' and ask the children to think of words that rhyme with it and write them on the board. Do the same with the word 'box'.

Writing activities

Objective Write things such as labels and captions (11). Use a pencil and hold it effectively to form recognisable letters (12).

You will need a worksheet with pictures of different packaging materials.

- Give out the worksheets and look at the pictures with the children. Ask them: *Do you think these things are waterproof?*
- Ask children to write the words 'Yes' or 'No' next to each item.

Assessment *(W, AF1)* Do the children think carefully before choosing their response?
(W, AF2) Do the children write legibly?

Fetch!

C = Language comprehension	*R, AF* = QCA reading assessment focus
W = Word recognition	*W, AF* = QCA writing assessment focus

Group or guided reading

Introducing the book

W Help the children to read the title, sounding out and blending the letters.

C *(Questioning, Prediction)* Ask the children: *What does 'fetch' mean? Who likes to fetch sticks? Do you think Floppy will fetch a stick?*

Strategy check

Remind the children to look carefully at the pictures to find out what is happening in the story.

Independent reading

C *(Questioning, Prediction)* Look at the first page of the story. Ask the children: *What are the dogs doing? Do you think Floppy will fetch a stick?*

C *(Prediction)* On pages 2–3, ask: *Do you think Floppy will fetch the stick Mum throws? Why do you think this?*

C *(Prediction)* On pages 4–5, ask: *Do you think Floppy will fetch the stick Biff throws? Why do you think this?*

C *(Questioning)* On pages 6–7, ask: *Why does Floppy suddenly dash into the water? Do you think he will fetch the stick?*

C *(Questioning, Imagining)* On page 8, ask: *What did Floppy fetch? What do you think Mum and the children said?*

C *(Summarising)* Ask the children to look through the book and tell the story in their own words.

Assessment Check that children:

- *(R, AF3)* use details from the illustrations to predict what will happen next.

Returning to the text

W Look at the word 'Fetch' on the cover. Ask the children: *What letter sound does it begin with? What letter sound does it end with?*

C *(Summarising)* Ask children to tell you whether the children in the story were pleased with Floppy in the end, and why.

Group and independent reading activities

Objective Show an understanding of the elements of stories, such as main character, sequence of events (7.3, 8.2).

C *(Questioning)* Ask the children:

Who is this story about?
Why do you think Floppy doesn't want to fetch the stick?
Why does Floppy fetch Biff's hat?
What words would you use to describe Floppy?

- Draw a picture of Floppy on the board and write some of the words that the children suggest to describe him around the picture.

Assessment *(R, AF3)* Do they empathise with the children in the story and understand why they are so pleased with Floppy?

Objective Recognise letter shapes and say a sound for each (5.3). Read some high frequency words (5.9).

W **You will need** character drawings of Mum, Biff, Chip, Floppy; cards with the names of the characters on them; reusable adhesive.

- Pin up pictures of the characters and ask the children to match the characters name to the correct picture.
- Write the following sentence on the board: 'Floppy is in the story.'

- Ask the children how many other characters there are in the story and write the sentence including their names.
- Ask the children to say the words in the sentence with you as you write them. Before reading the words 'is' and 'in', ask them to sound out and blend the letters in each word.

Assessment *(R, AF1)* Do the children read the correct word as you point to it?

Objective Recognise common digraphs (5.8).

W **You will need** cards with the following written on each: 'M', 'B', 'Ch', 'Fl', and a box.

- Write the characters' names on the board without their initial phonemes ('-um', '-iff', '-ip', '-loppy').
- Put the cards with the initial phonemes into a box and ask the children to choose a card.
- Ask the child to read the sound of the phoneme on the card and then try to match it with each of the final phonemes until the correct word is found.

Assessment *(R, AF1)* Do the children sound out the initial phonemes correctly?

Objective Use language to imagine and recreate roles and experiences (8.3).

C *(Imagining)* Ask the children to think of other words or phrases the children could have used to ask Floppy to get the stick, e.g. 'Please get it', 'Get it', 'Run after the stick!', 'Find it!'

- Discuss whether Floppy would have understood these words. Ask: *Would he have fetched the stick if the children had said 'please'?*

Assessment *(R, AF3)* Do the children think of some imaginative ideas, which are appropriate for the character of Floppy?

Speaking, listening and drama activities

Objective Enjoy listening to and using spoken and written language and readily turn to it in play and learning (1.1). Use language to imagine and recreate roles and experiences (4.1).

- Ask one child in the group to be Floppy. The other children ask 'Floppy' to fetch them something beginning with the phoneme 'm', 'b', 'ch' and 'f'.

Writing activities

Objective Attempt writing for various purposes (9.1). Use a pencil and hold it effectively to form recognisable letters (12).

- Help the children to draw four speech bubbles.
- Ask them to write 'Fetch!' in three of them, and 'Well done!' in the fourth.
- Help them to cut the speech bubbles out.
- Ask them to position the speech bubbles on the appropriate pages of the storybook.

Assessment *(W, AF2)* Do they use capital letters correctly and remember the exclamation mark?

(W, AF8) Do the children use correct spelling?

The Hedgehog

C = Language comprehension	*R, AF* = QCA reading assessment focus
W = Word recognition	*W, AF* = QCA writing assessment focus

Group or guided reading

Introducing the book

- Read the title and show the picture on the cover.
- C *(Questioning)* Ask the children: *What is a hedgehog? Can you show me the hedgehog on the cover? Where is the hedgehog?*

Strategy check

Check the children notice the characters' expressions and know that these show the characters' feelings.

Independent reading

- C *(Questioning)* Look at the first page of the story. Ask the children: *What are Biff and Floppy doing?*
- C *(Questioning, Clarifying)* On pages 2–3, ask the children: *What does Floppy find? How would you describe the hedgehog?*
- C *(Questioning, Clarifying)* On pages 4–5, ask: *Who can you see in the picture? Why is Floppy touching his nose?*
- C *(Questioning, Clarifying)* On pages 6–7, ask: *What time is it in the picture? How do you know? Where do you think Mum and the children are going?*
- C *(Questioning)* On page 8, ask: *What do you see? How would you describe the hedgehog in this picture?*
- C *(Summarising)* Ask the children to look through the book and tell the story in their own words.

Assessment Check that children:

- *(R, AF3)* scan the picture for details about the story
- *(R, AF3)* notice the change in time in the story and include this in their retelling.

Returning to the text

W Return to the title. Ask: *Can you see the small word in 'hedgehog'?* Cover 'hedge' and encourage them to sound out and blend the phonemes to read 'hog'. Cover up 'hog' and read 'hedge'.

C *(Imagining)* Turn to page 7 and ask: *Why do you think Mum kept Floppy inside?*

C *(Summarising)* Look at pages 3 and 8 and ask the children: *What is different about the hedgehog?* Ask them to explain why the hedgehog isn't like a ball at the end.

Group and independent reading activities

Objective Show an understanding of the elements of stories, such as main character, sequence of events, and openings (7.3).

C *(Clarifying)* Ask the children to show you a page where the story takes place during the day-time. Then ask if they can show you a page where the story takes place at night-time.

Assessment *(R, AF3)* Are the children able to refer to the right part of the book automatically?

Objective Explore and experiment with sounds, words and texts (5.1). Read texts compatible with their phonic knowledge and skills (5.12).

W **You will need** to write this sentence on the board: 'A hedgehog is in the garden.'

- Read the sentence with the children, pointing to each word as you say it.
- Ask the children to clap when they hear each word. Ask how many words there are in the sentence.

- Ask children to read the sentence aloud, pointing to each word as they say it.
- Substitute 'The hedgehog' for the characters' names and rewrite the sentence, asking the children to say the words with you as you write them.

Assessment *(R, AF1)* Do the children clap with each word? Make sure they do not clap with the rhythm of the words, just with each individual word.

Objective Extend their vocabulary, exploring the meanings and sounds of new words (1.5). Use phonic knowledge to write simple regular words (5.10).

W Write the word 'hog' on the board. Divide it into its phonemes 'h–o–g'.

- Ask the children to think of other words that rhyme with 'hog', e.g. 'dog', 'log'.
- Give the children a bag of initial phonemes. Ask them to take a card and read the phoneme. Can the children make some rhyming words with 'hog'?

Assessment *(R, AF1)* Can the children hear the rhyming pattern? Do the children correctly identify words and nonsense words?

Speaking, listening and drama activities

Objective Use talk to organise, sequence and clarify thinking, ideas, feelings and events (1.2).

- As a group, ask the children to look through the story and find three things they have learnt about hedgehogs from the story, e.g. *What do they look like? Where do they live? What do they do when they are scared? When do they come out?*
- Ask them to discuss why we don't often see hedgehogs.
- Ask them to think of other animals that only come out at night.

Writing activities

Objective Know that print carries meaning (7.1). Write their own names and other things such as labels and captions (11). Use a pencil and hold it effectively to form recognisable letters, most of which are correctly formed (12).

- Ask the children to draw a picture of a hedgehog and write the words 'The Hedgehog' underneath it. Tell them that they can copy the words from the front cover of the book.
- Ask the children to show you which is the picture and which is the writing.

Assessment *(W, AF8)* Do the children use correct spelling? Are the letters correctly formed?

The Apple

C = Language comprehension
W = Word recognition
R, AF = QCA reading assessment focus
W, AF = QCA writing assessment focus

Group or guided reading

Introducing the book

- Read the title and show the picture on the cover.
- C *(Questioning)* Ask the children: *Where is the apple? How many apples are on the tree? Why do you think Chip is pointing up at it?*
- C *(Prediction) Do you think they will get the last apple off the tree?*

Strategy check

Remind the children to look carefully at the pictures to see what is happening.

Independent reading

- C *(Questioning, Clarifying)* Look at the first page of the story. Ask the children: *What have the family been doing? How do you know? Why do you think they are looking at the apple? Do they want it?*
- C *(Questioning)* On pages 2–3, ask: *What is Dad doing? Can he reach the apple?*
- C *(Questioning)* On pages 4–5, ask: *What is Chip doing? Can he reach the apple?*
- C *(Questioning)* On pages 6–7, ask: *What happens to the apple? Who missed the apple? Who got the apple?*
- C *(Questioning, Imagining)* On page 8, ask: *What is Floppy doing? How does Dad feel? How does Kipper feel?*
- Ask the children to look through the book and tell the story in their own words.

Assessment *(R, AF3)* Check that children scan the picture for information and notice details such as the characters' expressions.

Returning to the text

W Point to the word 'Apple' on the cover. Can the children sound out the beginning phonemes?

W Look at the back cover and encourage the children to use their phonic knowledge to have a go at reading the question.

C *(Questioning, Clarifying)* Ask: *Who picked the last apple?* Look through the book to find the answer.

C *(Summarising)* Ask the children to tell you what happened in the story.

Group and independent reading activities

Objective Show an understanding of the elements of stories, such as main character, sequence of events, and openings (7.3). Retell narratives in the correct sequence (7.4).

C *(Questioning) Ask the children:*

What happened at the beginning of the story?

Who wanted the last apple on the tree?

How did they try to get the apple?

What happened when the apple fell down?

What happened at the end of the story?

Assessment *(R, AF3)* Do the children retell the story in the correct sequence?

Objective Begin to form simple sentences (11).

W **You will need** word cards for each of the characters' names and these words: 'wanted', 'the', 'apple'.

- Write this sentence on the board: 'Dad wanted the apple.'
- Ask the children to make new sentences using the characters' names and putting the word cards in the correct sequence to make the sentence.

Assessment *(W, AF6)* Do the children correctly sequence the words?

Objective Link sounds to letters, naming and sounding the letters of the alphabet (5.2).

- (W) Give each child a letter of the alphabet and ask them to think of a fruit which begins with that letter. Draw a picture of it and write the word underneath.
- Arrange the pages into alphabetical order to make a class alphabet book.

Assessment *(R, AF1)* Do the children correctly identify the initial letter of the fruit?

Speaking, listening and drama activities

Objective Use talk to organise, sequence and clarify thinking, ideas, feelings and events (1.2). Interact with others (3.1). Use language to imagine and recreate roles and experiences (8.3).

- Ask the children to say whether they like the ending of the story. Ask: *Do they think it was fair that Floppy got the apple? Who do they think should have got the apple?* Ask them to give reasons why.

Writing activities

Objective Use phonic knowledge to write simple regular words and make phonetically plausible attempts at more complex words (5.10). Attempt writing for various purposes (10).

- Ask the children to draw a picture of an apple tree and put labels on all the parts of it.

Assessment *(W, AF8)* Do their spelling attempts show phonic knowledge?

OXFORD
UNIVERSITY PRESS

Great Clarendon Street, Oxford OX2 6DP

Oxford University Press is a department of the University of Oxford. It furthers the University's objective of excellence in research, scholarship, and education by publishing worldwide in

Oxford New York
Auckland Cape Town Dar es Salaam Hong Kong Karachi
Kuala Lumpur Madrid Melbourne Mexico City Nairobi
New Delhi Shanghai Taipei Toronto

With offices in

Argentina Austria Brazil Chile Czech Republic France
Greece Guatemala Hungary Italy Japan Poland
Portugal Singapore South Korea Switzerland
Thailand Turkey Ukraine Vietnam

Oxford is a registered trade mark of Oxford University Press in the UK and in certain other countries

Written by Liz Miles, based on the original characters created by Roderick Hunt and Alex Brychta.

First published 2008
This edition published 2011

British Library Cataloguing in Publication Data

Data available

Cover illustrations Alex Brychta

ISBN: 978-0-19-848042-6

10 9 8 7 6 5 4 3 2 1

Page make-up by Thomson Digital

Printed in China by Imago

Paper used in the production of this book is a natural, recyclable product made from wood grown in sustainable forests. The manufacturing process conforms to the environmental regulations of the country of origin.